# A Sail to Great Island

# A Sail to Great Island

## Alan Feldman

The University of Wisconsin Press

The University of Wisconsin Press
1930 Monroe Street
Madison, Wisconsin 53711

www.wisc.edu/wisconsinpress/

3 Henrietta Street
London WC2E 8LU, England

5   4   3   2   1

Printed in the United States of America


Library of Congress Cataloging-in-Publication Data

Feldman, Alan, 1945–
A sail to great island / Alan Feldman.
p. cm.
ISBN 0-299-20260-7 (alk. paper)—ISBN 0-299-20264-X (pbk. : alk. paper)
I. Title.
PS3556.E458S25   2004
813'.54—dc22   2004012632

for Nan

# Contents

# III

# Acknowledgments

Thanks to the following publications where some of these poems previously appeared:

*Best American Poetry 2001*: "Contemporary American Poetry" (originally in *Poetry*)

*Denver Quarterly*: "Family Happiness"; "Old Post Card from the Jura"

*Iowa Review*: "A Visit from My Sister (c. 1982)"

*JAMA: Journal of the American Medical Association*: "After Watching Twyla Tharp"

*Kenyon Review*: "A Memoir"; "Dissolving the Boundaries"; "On the Mooring"

*Larcom Review*: "On Memorial Drive"

*Mediphors*: "For Sam"

*The Nation*: "A Visit from the Tree Man"; "Early Spring"

*North American Review*: "Self-Portrait"

*Poetry*: "Beside the Broad Dordogne"; "Bill Evans Plays *Never Let Me Go*"; "My Century"; "The Back of the Building"

*Press*: "Listening to Keats"

*Threepenny Review*: "Girls in the Museum"; "Reason"

*Virginia Quarterly Review*: "Pavane"; "This Fog"; "On Brattle Street"; "Girl with Sunflower in Hand"

I

# On the Mooring

This boat's like a little house that keeps turning
to look at things. Or else the houses go rolling by
on ball bearings, with their accompanying trees, then come
　　rolling back
as my boat swings on its mooring in Blackfish Creek.
Could someone invent a really complete camera, please,
that would catch everything, constantly, for just the time
I'd like to come back to, from time to time,
forever? Yes, it would have sound. The little fingers
of waves brushing the hull which sound
like a dog at a water bowl. And yes, ears
would register the rocking and swinging and the little scrapes
of wire rigging, the panting of the little sail, a "wind chute."
Maybe none of this is beautiful more than the rest
of the world, but a boat is a place
where all's tidy, stowed, and safe, even in the chaos
of a squall. Oh, Self, rereading this in winter,
close your eyes and listen. The south shore
of the creek just rolled across the transom, past
the tied tiller, its faded blue cover flapping.

# A Memoir

I'd like to write memoiristically, but my interest in myself
keeps getting in the way. Not to mention my foggy
memory. The miracle is you could describe your bedroom
at the corner of State Street. The low ceiling. The large
windows with their clear glass. And suddenly a place
rubs into focus, brighter than anything real,
and more lasting. Why brighter? Because in the present
we could be distracted by the camouflage pattern
of daily worry, gnawing at us like a hunger,
but in memory everything is bright and thought-about
like a painting with a frame that protects it
the way a wall protects a city. The city
of the past. I could write: *My mother*
*never shopped. Except to sit down at her narrow desk*
*and call the grocer, then the butcher, every morning*
*with her musical voice, as though she had to charm them*
*into delivering.* This is a sentence of memoir
and I am visible in every word of it, the overtone
of condemnation in the first, short declarative remark
and the jealousy of the final simile. My heart
is with the boy standing beside her, waiting for attention.
Oh, if I could only step outside, she could live again
and so could I. Forever, perhaps. That self-forgetfulness,
that turning oneself into a lens. That generous devotion.
I was the life my mother was planning to have
in her next life, I must have convinced myself.
And when I get into arguments, I find myself shouting
the way my grandfather would have. *Shouting*
*at board meetings was his amusement, rather than golf.*
Is that memoiristic? No, that shows my insane conviction
that the family dead return to life in me.

*for Miriam Levine*

4

# Listening to Keats

I could be listening to the news, but I'm listening to Keats
read by some honey-tongued young British actor
who, for all I know, might sound like Keats, his voice

lifted in pitch by my car's tape deck running fast.
I'm on a one-day news fast, if I can manage it—
one Tuesday where everything that happens will have to wait

till Wednesday for my response. And the Keats tape is important.
Mailed to me for my birthday from my daughter.
She was looking for tapes at Borders, and possibly recalled

my wistful relationship with Keats, seeing my mother—
dead lo these twenty years, once an English major—
weeping for Keats at the English Cemetery in Rome

when I was seven. I could read about it even now in her letters.
Keats, who sounds nothing like me. The mellifluous Keats
unbothered by the whine of trucks on the Massachusetts Turnpike,

Keats who could dance his syllables to a measure
while my lines are overcrowded like a mouth needing orthodontia.
For years I wouldn't read or read about Keats,

my mother's great love, now given to me by my daughter,
young enough to date Keats, who's twenty-five
(at most) forever. How he blazes with a love of love,

youth's great initial discovery, on moon-glinting St. Agnes Eve,
and feels, too, the fresh frost of early death,
his brain still teeming, no chance to set it all down.

And how he knows not to lift all his poems
to some grand sentiment, but to end with an image,
some forester in the cold—these poems in the porches of my ears.

How my mother must have loved him, since he could say
what my father couldn't: about a man's desperate love,
a woman's merciless beauty. My father who called to chat

on the day that happened to be my birthday, but couldn't just say
Happy Birthday. Or didn't remember. So, hey, I said it for him,
I wouldn't change him. Or anything else at this moment,

except to have my daughter nearer, though I feel near to her
listening to Keats. My mother, my daughter, and me,
passing trucks, going through the toll booths,

the dead Keats reading passionately, deathlessly.

# Pavane

The first time I heard Ravel's *Pavane for a Dead Princess*
I was in band practice at Lawrence High School. Our stands
held the dog-eared parts—Horn 1 & 2 and Solo Horn,
which George Gellis got to play so soulfully
that Sue Meyer, Jane Furchgott, and I hated to add
our uncertain sound. Some days I was in love with Jane
who was angelically pretty but had an acne problem.
And Sue was my friend, the older sister I'd gladly have traded
my real sister for. The first time I heard that melody
glide like a river of silk out of George Gellis's horn
I couldn't understand how it had been given to an arrogant senior,
who either despised or simply ignored me, to say
the saddest, most beautiful thing that had ever been said.
How could he know it, or translate it off the page?
And I never envied anything more than to play that melody
with that sound as if George had been sheathed in golden armor
and I, with a few bars of accompaniment, was his page.

Music aside, I wanted a sorrow that mournful
for my own. And two years later, when Sue
went off to college and died freshman year
falling through the ice at a school camp in northern Michigan
while walking across the lake at night with her boyfriend,
I would sit at the piano and swoon out that *Pavane*.
Always it brought her back to me, and I count up my life
since I was seventeen, the age she died,
as though I could answer her last letter to me again.
She came to my room once, to talk to me about my crush on Jane,
as though she might have had a crush on me. Unreasonable,
but what if we'd started to make out? Would she have been walking
     with someone
so late that icy night? Out flow the bars of the *Pavane*,
George Gellis's one reason for being in the world.

She must be a young favorite there in the world of the dead—
so level-headed, yet idealistic. If I could write to her,
answering the card with the Japanese print of men in the snow
that I keep inside *New Directions 16*, a volume she inscribed to me,
I'd begin, Sue, I think of you whenever I hear the Ravel piece,
as though it marks your grave (wherever in Michigan that is).
If Jane's still alive, and if she still thinks of you,
that would make two of us who remember the day
when Mr. Jones, on a dull afternoon, as though
he wanted to hear George Gellis play just once
before he graduated (knowing he'd only have the three of us
left in the horn section next year), passed out
the band version of Ravel's *Pavane*, and George
(a musician who, as far as I know, had no feelings)
filled the Lawrence High auditorium with somber beauty.

You must have joined the rest of us to accompany him,
none of us managing to be any more in-tune than usual,
with those dented instruments we'd borrowed
from the school's storeroom. But it seemed to me
(as it does today) that I'd always remember you—
how, with Jane and me, when our cues came,
you put your lips to your horn
and blew the spirit of your life into that music.

# Beside the Broad Dordogne

I wake to the sound of water, and think,
"Mother has died and gone to France."
She is at *un autre hôtel*, speaking French
better than ever, while I stare at the fog
that has a river in it—the broad Dordogne,
making its river noise, as if all the faucets
have been left on all night. The river
rushing in one direction only, so different
from Blackfish Creek, where the sea floods in
and back, scrubbing the sand both ways.

Well, one travels so things are different.
American actors speak French on TV here.
Last night I watched *Accident Catastrophe*
about two babies switched in the hospital at birth.
One dies. The parents discover the dead child
was someone else's and their child is alive
in Florida with *son père*, though *sa mère*
*est morte de* some disease, who knows?

Anyway, Ed Asner, who plays the lawyer,
speaks gravelly French, but people have
an American demeanor, they pull their hair
on the edge of violence. Then each family
gives up a piece, and the child ends up more
loved than ever, as if it's inevitable.
Or so the river is telling me
with its one-way simplicity,
like gravity. "Alive in the eternal
heart of France"—that's Mother
I'm thinking about, for some reason,

maybe the journal my wife's been keeping,
so like the daily letters Mother wrote

to *sa mère et son père*, when her life
was flowing through her like the broad
Dordogne. And where is she now?
Does she wish my father were with her,
one of him alive, and one with her?
A bell is ringing wildly, each of its peals
like a round boat rolling downstream
where the river divides around an island
only to sweep back into itself
somewhere in the fog.

# A Visit from My Sister (c. 1982)

She gets off the bus in my mother's old mink coat
and dungarees. Carrying a flight bag. She's made a quick
circle around the country. Has even seen our remote
father in Florida. Two of her friends are widows.
We're getting older and older. Luckily. I don't
feel like lecturing her about her unfinished dissertation.
I accept everything. Even her ice cream dinners. I won't
back my father when he accuses her of procrastination
and worries how she'll collect social security in Istanbul.
Are you happy? is all I ask her when we talk.
"Mmm, yes . . ." she says, considering. Her eyes full.
She shows me a photo of the view from her balcony. A short walk
along the Bosporus brings her to the ferry that goes
to Asia. It's sunny. The wind ruffles her clothing.

# On Memorial Drive

Watching the river, an orchestra playing a fugue,
while I wait for my parking space to be legal,
writing my poem, while a river of cars
plunges by in tumbling waves and the placid
water river beside it moves in little ripples
like the slow movement on the radio
now. Still on earth. The little balls
on the sycamores (where the bark
peels in piebald patterns) tremble, hanging on.
Still here. The trees still reaching their nerve-endings
across the blue sky with its orderly streams
of boxcar-shaped clouds. Oh earthly stream
in which I myself usually travel, but today
I'm a living stone, a man in a parked car
under the piebald trees, listening
to the sighing of the tires, catching the silver skin
of the river, its prickles of light, in the side-view mirror,
shedding my business cares like a man turning up
the volume of his music-thoughts to drown out
the declarative and interrogative sentences
of his prosy head, his heart sitting quietly
in his chest, for once, his heart singing and breathing
like a cello, oh to be irresponsible, but never lonely . . .

So turn up the music, as if in childhood,
waiting for Mother to show up after school,
waiting beneath the flaking sycamores,
while cars with wrap-around windshields cruise by
until I'm the last kid left, getting to know
the maps of the tree trunks, to peel the pieces
from the limbs, and study the bark
with an empty brain, or split open
the little balls with my thumb
and shake into the wind
the fuzz of a million seeds.

# Woman

*A woman is a sometime thing*, Satchmo sings
on Christopher's copy of the *Porgy and Bess* Satch
made with Ella Fitzgerald. We're back
from a day at the *plage* at Cassis.
All those breasts bared to the sun,
the melons, the ripe strawberries,
*oh, a woman is a sometime thing,* like strawberries
if they're in season. This woman
in my life could slip out of my life

which is why Christopher's photos
haunt me at first, and not just
the sad ones, Sabine
in her exotic headdresses
(to cover thin or absent hair),
but even the one in the kitchen,
Sabine with bread and butter before her,
smiling with love at Christopher,
her hair pinned back carelessly,
since love has or has not ended.
(Is death an end to love?)

*Oh, a woman is a sometime thing*, and a man
too, and the happy conjunction of love.
To taste this fruit means a kind of knowledge,
Satchmo is telling us. *A woman is,*
and someday may not be,
but a woman is delicious,
his hungry, experienced voice
is telling us, *Oh, a woman
is a sometime thing,* like the light,
like the day, the one and only day

with this woman at that beach
the clouds will not revisit, not
those same clouds, not those same
rays of ultraviolet and visible light,
not the same look of love
on the woman's face, as she sighs
with pleasure.

# Dissolving the Boundaries

Book report: Have you read R. K. Narayan's *The English Teacher?*
You may recall, it's about a man's adjustment to living with his wife
after he's gotten used to solitude. At first he treats her
as a nuisance. Then he begins to defer. Would she like
a bigger house? Too late. She dies. This is India
but it's the same as here. Everyone expects him to remarry
but he doesn't. Instead he finds that if he can think of her
with the right sort of receptive mind, her thoughts can carry
messages across the death barrier. At the end
she's sitting on his bed in her sky-blue sari. It's strange
but not so strange. It takes a certain effort to bend
but then there's a fusion. I found the story beautiful. People are
    ashamed
to love so exclusively. Be tough, they say. Accept your losses.
Life is just a stagecoach ride, and your lovers are the horses.

# Contemporary American Poetry

When her eye first gave her trouble, but when I did not yet know
this growth would spread through her brain, Mother sent me
Donald Hall's "Kicking the Leaves," torn from the *Times*,

one of the clippings that piled up around her feet while she read
to scout out the news for half-a-dozen people,
but particularly for her children, particularly for me.

Hall—so uncool—in a poem so humble and conventional,
where the leaves are dying leaves, not pie plates,
and stand for what we always know they stand for.

In a way, this poem was my mother's leave-taking,
what she would have said to me if she wrote poems.
*My darling*, she tried to say, through Hall's poem,

*I will soon be leaving you. When you hear about my death
you will be staring at a blood red leaf against a raw blue
October sky through a film of tears, and you will be*

*an orphan. The price you will have to pay
for having been loved—essentially without qualification—
by me. I am leaving you now with this clipping,*

*this poem about leaves from the editorial page of the* Times,
*which I read daily, always with thoughts of you.*
How I resented this poem, which moved me terribly,

though it was completely without jokes or irony,
unadorned and sad as a New England graveyard,
the anthem of our family, not designed for tragedy,

other than the loss of each other, my mother signaling to me
through the voice of her bearded Protestant avatar:
*I diminish, not them, as I go first into the leaves*

*taking the step they will follow, Octobers and years from now.*
Mother, you'd be eighty-four, though younger than some of my
    students.
Like them, you'd listen skeptically to my praise for my contemporaries

like Louise Glück. *Her mother, Bea, went to high school with me*
*in the Twenties. She's added the umlaut. Remember*
*her paintings at the library when she just got out of the hospital?*

*See, dear, you were never troubled or gloomy enough to be a poet,*
*though, like Donald Hall, you have and will have losses.*
*Remember his poem about the leaves? I sent you a clipping once,*

*though I know you always threw out my clippings.*
*Still, I sent them, messages for you piling up around my feet*
*each night as I sat and read the* Times *and thought of you.*

Now the poem's in our *Contemporary American Poetry* anthology,
one that puts old enemies, like O'Hara and Lowell, together
in an academy of poetry of the world to come.

And Hall, who looks healthy now, also had cancer,
and nearly died, but here he's still in his mid-forties,
happy his long drought is over and he's writing again.

He's kicking the leaves, leaping and exultant, recovering from death,
and I am rereading his poem, thinking of myself at thirty,
scornful and envious, moved and suspicious, reading in his poem,

one of the few my mother ever cared to send me,
about what he calls *the pleasure, the only long pleasure*
*of taking a place in the story of leaves,* which is one hundred percent

grief. The pleasure, if there is one, is knowing we have the dead
inside us, where they have to make peace, and never leave us.
My mother, in class today, though dead way back,

will go home to hang her coat in the closet of heaven and say:
*What a wonderful class! I don't like much in contemporary American poetry,*
*except for "Kicking the Leaves" by Donald Hall. But the teacher—*

*he's like that Louis Rukeyser on* Wall $treet Week
*I watch faithfully, though I leave the investing to Barney.*
*A man like that—anything he says is worth listening to.*

# Girl with Sunflower in Hand

Holding a sunflower in a forties magazine,
a blonde with a yellow scarf knotted around her neck
like a scout's neckerchief, an American girl,
say twenty, the sunflower held before her like a hand mirror
she turns away from. No flower needs to tell her
she's pretty. Her shining hair pinned back. Her brow
so smooth light seems to be coming from it.
Her sweater is a gray so soft it has pinks in it
and the softest yellows. Her eyes are the gray-blue of water.

American because she's against no background
except smoky gray, brown, and deep blue,
perhaps the steam of a train. A girl
from my mother's era whose job it is to be the sun
for others. But she can do this and stand alone.
Her own roots. Her own stalk. Her sun
somewhere above and to the left, burning through haze.

Back then my mother liked to doodle pretty faces
while she chatted on the phone, the profiles of perfect women,
though now I know they were like this sunflower girl,
the girl my mother never was, but is now,
in death, where she hears music whenever she wishes,
a pretty American girl who knows only hope
that flows into her hair like gold. So odd that the soul
is so bodiless it can flow like gray stuff which isn't gray at all
around a body like a sweater. On the face of the sunflower
there are hundreds of seeds. In the life she has now
each idea my mother has becomes human,
the way I did years ago, my hair light gold.

A soul is what you can look like forever if you wish,
the way sunflowers keep coming back in whole fields
of perfect beings, perfect loving beings
that bloom and rejoin the sun.

# II

# Family Happiness

**1.**

Family happiness is never complete
because they all go off in a van,
my daughter driving like Mister Magoo,
and I have to wonder if I *have* a family.
At this very moment they could be sailing
to heaven, the rock music they love blaring.
Which is why—Tolstoy or not—
marriage is never boring, why it's like sailing,
even the smooth motion deceptive, a balance
of hellish forces. Make one stupid turn
and see the fluid you were gliding in
is really a storm.

**2.**

I'm writing this on my front porch, out of danger,
with nobody home, the whole hillside
swept by wind, the pines nodding in place
the way I used to see men swaying
in synagogue, praying.
The air is passing over my skin,
some Windham Hill yuppie music is on the hi fi.
Everything's breezy, the music says.
My bible lies by my side, *The Complete Guide
to Sailing, Cruising and Racing.*
I keep it next to my corn flakes
and bananas each morning. Capsizing, it says,
shows that you're pushing the limits of your craft.
I try to keep everything tinkling
and jingling along like George Winston
and his piano, as interesting as watching leaves rustle.

Should I lean right out of the boat and fight
if it's a strong breeze, say seven Beaufort,
which is like a fierce scherzo by Beethoven,
all ten fingers busy grabbing
everything they can hold on to?

**3.**

If all marriages are tragedies (because they end)
how are we supposed to take a comic perspective,
make life end in a marriage?
The boats sail, like little white shark's teeth,
and I hear from the neighboring cottage:
*"I've* come up with *all* the suggestions
and *nobody* wants to do what *I* want to do.
So now *you* make the suggestions."
Just another storm in the cottages
while the sea is calm.

# Girls in the Museum

Friday morning the museum is overrun with teenage girls. From
  a school
where sweaters with bright winter scenes seem to be in fashion.
Now they're on a different kind of shopping expedition. "That's
  pretty," one of them says
when they pass *The Daughters of Edward D. Boit.*
Does she mean the girls in the painting? The Boits' paneled living
  room? Or the big vases beneath which the girls seem so tiny?
On the bench in front of the painting two more girls are deep in
  conversation,
talking about when it's morally permissible to break the law,
while two others are trying to connect Euclidean geometry and the
  immortality of the soul.
Where does such talk come from?
As though at fifteen the brain starts to bubble like soda
and all of these ideas are coming into being for the first time.

Their teacher tells them about the Boits' enormous vases
that crossed the ocean seventeen times: Cleaned for a recent showing
they dislodged dance cards, ping pong balls, stale donuts—
debris as miscellaneous as the mind's.
She's showing them the way the cinnabar screen points to the
  four-year-old
like an exclamation point. How fast they grow! The eight-year-old
  fidgets.
The twelve-year-old looks as though she might lift one of her gangly
  arms
to wave. And the fourteen-year-old leans back against a vase
in profile, her pale cheek inscrutable as marble.

Down the hall the girls crowd around Degas' *Little Dancer Fourteen
  Years Old.*
A squint of ecstasy on her face, little worker!

Maybe they pity her? The way she either makes it into the corps or
    it's back to the sweatshop?
Her neck extended, her arms forced back behind her,
she holds her awkward pose for the centuries to look at her
and gives herself to beauty like a soldier.

# Self-Portrait

Near the door, Van Gogh's face glows like a moon,
an aura of green light centered on the right eye.
A mud-colored, impasto coat. Lapels of electric blue.
A purple clot near his collar. It's not a tie
or a flower. Maybe it's meant to be a broach
or an unhealed wound. If we start with a button
on his vest, move up to the eyes, we approach
the idea of a man as a constellation. Whatever he suffers
can't be personal. Forehead like a headlight, he stares at us
steady, pale green. "You perish," he tells us,
broadcasting his single-frequency message. "What matters
is that everything blazes away to its dust
in pain. Take it from me. Or my green wall.
You're born. Trees wave their wild arms. And that's all."

# For Sam

I wish you'd remembered to zip your shorts
when you walked to the other side of the pool
to tell me: *A man said "I have good news*
*and bad news. First do you want to hear*
*the good news?" And the man says*
*"My wife is leaving me."* Someone near me
has an awful, hacking cough. Puddles
on the pool deck. I wish you would put in
your lower teeth. The ones you have are like pickets
in a wrecked fence. Each smile startles me.

*"So what's the bad news?"* His thighs are thinner
than some fat people's arms. Like a flamingo
he miraculously still walks on his thin legs.
In the pool the slow swimmers drift like weeds,
like clothing fallen overboard. The old ones
cluster in club chairs, watching the water walkers.
Is he depressed because he can't remember?
Or is his memory faltering because he's depressed?
This is not yet an elegy. So many creases
coming from the eyes. *"The bad news?"*
He carries the joke to me like water cupped in his hands.

Oh Sam, I know the punch line. How you tripped
on the stairs and your wife of fifty years
shrieked, as though you'd fallen from a train.
The eyes seem clear. *"The bad news is . . ."*
Your arm skin is brown as a turkey drumstick.
The bad news is that the only good news
is a stay of bad news. *"She changed her mind!"*
*That's the joke that fellow there told me.*
A momentary stay against confusion.
Oh stay. Don't wade across the pool.

This is not yet an elegy. When did you start
flailing at net shots? How long before my thighs
become as thin as yours in a room like this one
with my wife losing her grip on her patience
and a younger friend looking now at me and now away.

# At the Château Noir

You've all seen it—even if you don't know you have—
in the landscapes of Cézanne, a square of bright stone
with pointed gothic windows.

For Cézanne, all art came from feeling.
He tried church, but hated the curé's singing voice,
which left him with only circles, cylinders, cubes.

Don't think life is idyllic here. Cézanne
was given to shocking tantrums. He thought it patriotic
to condemn Dreyfus, whom Zola, his childhood friend,
championed at personal risk, cursed by children
as they walked by the window on his Paris street.

If Nan doesn't urge me to drive into the ancient, confusing town,
I'll have some time—first in weeks—to write.

Please don't think we're simply happy.
Even after Nan promised not to be here a few hours,
she just walked into the room and unzipped a suitcase.

"Leave," I tell her, seething. "Go paint something.
Weren't you talking about the olives with their silvery leaves?"

When Cézanne wasn't getting anywhere
he'd stab his canvases, then hurl them
out the window, into the trees.

"You're a square," he said to that building.
"You're feathery," he said to the trees.

"You," I say to my feelings, "are feathery. But you,"
I say to my feelings, "are shaped like a mountain,

always to be there." Just walk up the hill
and you'll recognize the profile of that mountain.
How many times Cézanne painted it—
often with branches in the foreground
that must have been swaying.

# Using Anne Frank

If I were like her, a better person,
I'd count this moment a blessing—
sitting on a terrace in the Drôme
while the sky refuses to make up its mind—
deep clouds one moment, then annoying sun
forcing me to move my chair into shade.
And I wouldn't be disturbed
by my stomach grumbling for lunch,
or the highway breathing so loudly
with the sounds of traffic as it leads
to the city from our little town.

But the person I am needs to imagine
giving this moment to her as a gift
to value it. How irises and roses
crowding the edge of the lichen-flecked wall
would have exploded as a gift to her weak eyes
after years in an attic with only windows
to sneak a look through, and at safe times only.

While the mountains lie sleeping under their green blankets,
we'd talk about the only subject we should care about,
whether life itself is the gift, the more the better,
or whether we're meant to have it
framed by the black frame of death,
the way goodness is so moving here
in this world—since it's not the norm—
though she says she thinks it is,
from what she's seen in her brief time.

# In My Dream I Appear before the Senate

Nobody's truly bad here, or didn't start that way.
Imagine we could go back to what we were—
the president's attorney could rise out of his wheelchair,
the president could come over in a T-shirt, and we'd set up the bases
    on the capitol lawn.
Not like now, with him visible only on television with his pancake
    makeup,
and his bullet-proof suit, and his words sincere and calculated to
    please.

In summer camp, in our bunks at night, under our blankets,
we might have dreamed of being the athletes we couldn't be in the
    daytime,
not boys different from ourselves, but boys made from highlights,
our best moves. And, when sex came into our world,
it was without context: maybe a girl in a training bra
offering us her suntanned body in a dream,
the way the summer offered us the sun, the diamond, the oiled-
    leather
smell of a mitt, the klock of a hardball against a Louisville Slugger.

Back then everyone had a self (vague) and a baseball self:
We knew who threw side-arm, and who, if nervous, was apt to throw
    wild.
The president would throw me a ball.
It would whack into the pocket of my glove,
stinging my hand, both of us really there under the flickering trees.

When camp was over, we'd go back to different lives. In my dream
    now
I stand in front of the Senate: Let's have some pity here.
Imagine if you gave everything to public life? In the dense night
of the central office of the world, your body wakes up, hums, tells
    you you're human.

But you don't kill anyone, or steal things. Remember back in camp?
The weird kid who arranged mice in pyramids behind the crafts
    shop?
Oh he was never caught, but we knew who did it,
and he went home as friendless as he came in June.

# On Brattle Street

It's sunny, but fat flakes of snow
are swirling in the air on Brattle Street
outside the library window where he sits
hoping to answer, in the spare hour he has,
a woman friend's challenging remark
that few men allow themselves to listen
to an inner voice of prophecy.
Fat flakes, as if the people on the sidewalk,
and the theater with its bright banners,
and the stick-like trees, are all within a paperweight
and even his doubts are a bubble world
within the star-choked larger universe,
and perturbation is no more than the shaking
of the little glass globe, the flakes already settling
once again on the roofs of the houses.

How pathetic that he can't remember when the gods in him
were last heard from, when they last seized control.
Maybe he should look at himself laughing and talking, losing
   himself
within the pleasant duties of daily sociability,
to understand what his genes always had in mind for him,
affable, as his grandfather was,
and round-bellied, now, like the Chinese god of prosperity?

Sometimes, when he is knotted in a knit tie, and seems least free,
at a meeting interrupted by a note and a messenger,
and he signs something, e-mails an answer, the phone rings,
and everything is happening at once, and nothing seems worth
   remembering,
he finds no inner voice at all, no gap between reflection and speech,

as if his whole life has been a cowardly deafness to the true song
that is filling Brattle Street beyond the library's glass wall.
Though it doesn't stir the banners on the theater,
or dislodge the plaster casts of snow from the trees,
it floods the brains of some of the sidewalk-trudgers passing by
who may not know whether the wordless song they hear
is one of longing, or of praise.

# The Back of the Building

None of the paintings Nan has done of our apartment
shows the view from our kitchen window.
Though our kitchen is all window. A kind of greenhouse
tacked onto the back of a West 4th Street brownstone.
Did you know that between the buildings on 12th Street
and the buildings on Bank Street there's a series of yards
we overlook? Imagine stockade fences, mini-
basketball hoops for juniors, a painting studio,
garden hoses, barbecues covered with tarps,
sooty lawn chairs, and trees rising a bit higher than the buildings
covered with ivy to about the third story.
Yes. Right here in Manhattan. Where the ground's so precious.

The six-story building on Bank Street has a blank wall,
beige and blank, on which ivy is growing nearly to the top.
No, it is not in leaf yet. This is only March,
and when it's green we will be gone. What it is now
is whorls of clinging tendrils, complicated as nerve cells,
crossed by the shadow of a tree which looks like an artery system.
It all gets simpler at the top. Just beige cement
with an occasional exposed brick. Let me
give you the address: 309 West 4th Street.

The apartment is on the second floor. It's owned
by Frieda M. Silvert, who's in her seventies. It could be,
by the time you're reading this she will have sold the building—
a tiny one, but probably worth millions.
Realtors call all the time. "No, this isn't Frieda,"
says Nan. "Frieda's traveling." "No, this isn't
Mr. Silvert," I say. "He's gone." I'm telling you
these details, though, in case you ever find yourself walking
on West 4th Street. You'll see 309 above the transom
of a beveled glass doorway. And now you'll know
what's in back of the building, and who's been living here.

Next you should go to 240 West 10th Street
and gaze up at the morbid, sunset-colored,
deep-red-brick façade with its many windows.
Here, in 1951, Frank O'Hara and a few friends
pretended to listen to Kenneth Koch on the wonders of Europe,
where Frank had not yet been, and would not yet go,
till the Museum of Modern Art sent him
to Spain to arrange a show. So?—he kept thinking—
So? All he needed was here. His million friends.
The sunlight in the gorges and canyons. What couldn't grow
right here where millions were exhaling so trees could breathe?

Nothing. Everything is here. In the kitchen
Frieda has a small tree which has been shedding its leaves,
though each day the sun (if there is sun) rises higher
above the six-story building on Bank Street.
I wish we could stay to watch the leaves
break out all over that blank beige wall facing our kitchen,
and walk once more to the Art Greenwich movie theater,
where *Rushmore* and *Forces of Nature* are playing—
which O'Hara would say is all the nature we need.

# Old Post Card from the Jura

Those are the cows clanking in the dark. They stay out
all night in summer, their bells beating like rigging
on aluminum masts. Across the valley with its model-railroad houses
we heard, this afternoon, a gasoline bandsaw singing
in the village square cutting stovewood. And all their water
is rainwater collected from roof gutters into cisterns
underground. It tastes sweet. I thought
I saw the old man tending his garden turn
to watch us stepping through the churchyard crowded with stones
on the last ledge of the village. The skull and crossbones
above our heads said: Respect these remains
as you would your own. Of course we want to stay.
What a view here on this mountain where even
the water circulating in the central heating comes from heaven.

# Sailing Solo

It gives me a glimpse of another life. You'd think
it's solitary, anchored at a distance from other boats,
my floppy sunbleached hat over my eyes,
the little houses set on shore, two tiny steeples
above the fluffy green of the trees. But it's not.
I've had a visitor, a man a little older than myself,
a gold anchor nestled in his white chest hairs.
He circled me in a beat-up runabout,
rocked me awake with his wake. Wanted to know
how long is that boat? I thought I was trespassing.
It turned out he owns a boat of the same unusual kind.
English. Tough, but almost extinct. The same
two keels so it can stand on its own two feet.
He told me the good anchorages around here for us,
where those with boats like ours—only like ours—
can go and can't be followed. Whenever such a boat
comes into his harbor he likes to visit it.
I imagine him with his eye all the time on the sea.
If he has family, he doesn't mention them,
only a brother (who owns a different sort of boat).
I mention my son, only to say it's good
the door to our front cabin closes, since Dan snores.
Perhaps there are no women in this world.
No sexes. Just the boats, which are neuter
and keep a discreet distance, as they pivot
more or less in synch on their moorings.
This is the place age brings you, back before boyhood,
an infant rocking, rocking, enfolded by its love,
the way the sea makes a curved round space
for my boat and for me. It's not that no one can reach me.

But when they do they seem to talk about passages
I've yet to take. Out here the screams of children
trapped in temporary, volcanic misery in vacation cottages
still reach. Louder is the gull's searching cry.
*Here?* he's asking. If you take desire away
does that leave peace? No, even the boat knows,
as it rattles its halyards in a puff of breeze.

# By the Time I Met Brian's Father

He was wasted to a terrifying thinness, his hands
weak, his voice silenced by a breathing tube,
so he could only write brief sentences, his eyes
astounded by his helplessness, his brain ringing
with anger, his feet restless and in pain, a TV
blaring nothing and nothing and more nothing.
And we were all around his bedside: Nan,
and Dan, and Becky, and Brian, her fiancé,
and when my turn came I stood over him,
feeling monstrous with good health, touched him,
and told him I knew how proud he was
of Brian, his son. He summoned
a pencil, and slowly, like an airplane forming
a letter at a time across the sky,
he wrote that he was hanging in there
to see their happiness. He was seeing
their wedding every time he looked at them.
He was speaking with the single syllable
of his love for them. *We pass,* he said.
*But look how worthy they are, how sane*
*and loving and worthy, as they stand*
*with the sun on their faces,*
*and have our eyes and our hair.*

# I Come Back from a Sail

It's December, and no one would want to sail
up here in New England—no one, that is, who's sane—
though sanity's not a requirement for sailors. The sea
doesn't care, sloshing or raging against the same shore
as in summer, but the fierce wind, cold as steel,
makes most of us huddle beside a fire on land.

Sometimes I wonder what it would be like to land
on Jeremy Point at a time like this—not a sail
on the razor edge of the horizon, or on the blue steel
of the bay. What does it matter, staying sane,
when my thoughts drift away from words towards the shore
of dreams, or captionless pictures, my ears ringing with the sea

wind that makes the island's grasses wild. Only at sea
does the brain become what confronts it, the waves that land
on the foredeck, the sheets in my hand. It shores
me up, when I'm scattered. I come back from a sail,
feel nothing's complicated, and that I'm sane
even if the world's not. It's as if sleep's been stealing

over me. Or not sleep. My bones turning to steel
so I can't be rattled. I suppose I love the sea,
though I fear it. Or because I do. It's sane
to get scared by the force of it, unimaginable on land,
the cruelty of the gale snapping the loose sail
like a whip. And the hopeless distance to the shore

that must be crossed to get out of its grip. On shore
it's difficult to guess how vast, pitiless, and steely
those forces can be. But try going out under sail,

even double-reefed. I've seen the sea
milk-white, the air so full of sleet the land's
another universe. I suppose it's insane

to be out there. But I guess it's sane
to know what we're up against. If you stay on shore
you have to strain to listen, the gods on land
not often speaking above a whisper. But off-shore
in the cold, steel claws of terror, they roar.

# To Solitude

*Oh, let me swim a little, will you?* That's what a woman said
at the pond yesterday. *Oh, Michael, let me swim a little,*
and she actually swam ahead and left him paddling
his thin arms and legs. He wasn't wearing a life-vest.
The water was deep enough to disappear into blurry blackness
from which it's hard to recover bodies. She swam ahead
and I kept an eye on the kid. Solitude,
there's only so much of you on earth to go around,
but I don't want anyone dying on your account.
In some other place I'll write about the union of bodies
dancing at my daughter's wedding, or the guests from out of town,
not yet gone, but just now I'm thinking of my scary
pent up need to be apart. They're off to the flea market
for the morning. I thought I'd stay in the deserted house,
let my coffee steam up into the silence like an offering
to you, my shameful love, and summon you, hoping
you'll stay with me, and won't go off by yourself, leaving me
with flat emptiness, the busy bread maker paddling its dough,
the shouting brightness of my wife's paintings reproaching me
for missing out on the flea market. But no, you're here.
You've come off your boat to be with me, and will find me,
from time to time, even for a brief kiss during a wedding,
when everyone's whirling around, and I hear you whispering.

# Bill Evans Plays *Never Let Me Go*

*Never let me go*, says the piano,
then the five syllables are repeated
a little lower, maybe more sadly,
or with more acceptance that this plaint
is endless, fruitless, but it is the plaint
of love forever, whatever else changes,
and the five notes always sound different
the way the lover constantly is finding
new ways to ask what can't be answered.
The piano takes a break to think it over
all around the keyboard, as if it is free
to take a walk, anywhere away from
those five notes, but no, it's been walking
towards them. *Never let me go,*
it says cheerfully, tenderly, without reproach,
as if it knows that saying so is its true calling.

III

# This Fog

I'm lost in fog. Not metaphorically.
Not in the middle of life's journey. But midway
between green can "8" and Hadley Harbor,
which should be beyond that colorless all-color
that might as well be the edge of the earth. I cling
to the one gray-black rocky finger of land
included in the mortal circle I can see.
Depth should be four feet or better to the west of that
so I'll drop anchor as soon as I get there,
and wait forever, not sailing and motoring
against a current fast enough to make green can "8"
look like the smokestack of a drowned steamer
going full speed ahead even as it's sinking.
Oh God, I think, though I do not think I believe
in petitionary prayer. The sea is bigger than I am,
and I always do something to reawaken a sense of contingency.
What can I say? My voice to the living
would sound pathetic and posthumous as the cockpit voice recorder
recovered from crashes, or the too-human postures
of the charcoal-colored Mt. Vesuvius victims
reaching for help, still, after two thousand years.
So, by the compass, I'm going to have to save myself,
believe in my belief that's Timmy Point,
no parent or instructor to nod a calm confirmation,
lower an anchor, and hope the one rock I can see,
shaped like an anvil, isn't taken from me too
by this fog. This fog which, if I live, will soon be metaphor.

# Reason

In the version of the play I'm watching, Antigone
goes to her death, just as in your version,
and Creon, in the name of the state, has lost
his heir. But in my version a god sings a song
that entrances everyone, so all of them know
they've been a part of a music they had no notion of,

or so sings the god who comes into the theater.
As a song has a beat, and a changing and repeating rhythm,
so the body has a heart, and an adaptable mind.
While the mind causes errors, often provoked by the heart,
the mind insists on speaking, even metrically,
and so we go to our deaths: articulate, and in error,

formidable, deserving of awe, and odd—
as the chorus seems to know. Watch our dance
of custom and ceremony. Creon should listen to us:
Bury the dead, as our city's ritual prescribes.
And Antigone, obey our king, and end this story,
so our fear won't overwhelm even our pity.

Sweet Reason, all that's needed to make peace among us.
Creon's desire for a triumphant city, and Antigone's
love for the dead, who alone cannot betray her—
no wonder our hearts are divided, as if by a knife.
The song has its reasons but is outside of reason
for the usual reasons, or so sings the god.

# My Century

The year I was born the atomic bomb went off.
Here I'd just begun, and someone
found the switch to turn off the world.

In the furnace-light, in the central solar fire
of that heat lamp, the future got very finite,
and it was possible to imagine time-travelers

failing to arrive, because there was no time
to arrive in. Inside the clock in the hall
heavy brass cylinders descended.

Tick-tock, the chimes changed their tune
one phrase at a time. The bomb became
a film star, its glamorous globe of smoke

searing the faces of men in beach chairs.
Someone threw up every day at school.
No time to worry about collective death,

when life itself was permeated by ordeals.
And so we grew up accepting things.
In bio we learned there were particles

cruising through us like whales through archipelagoes,
and in civics that if Hitler had gotten the bomb
he'd have used it on the inferior races,

and all this time love was etching its scars
on our skins like maps. The heavens
remained pure, except for little white slits

on the perfect blue skin that planes cut
in the icy upper air, like needles sewing.
From one, a tiny seed might fall

that would make a sun on earth.
And so the century passed, with me still in it,
books waiting on the shelves to become cinders,

what we felt locked up inside, waiting to be read,
down the long corridor of time. I was born
the year the bomb exploded. Twice

whole cities were charred like cities in the Bible,
but we didn't look back. We went on thinking
we could go on, our shapes the same,

darkened now against a background lit by fire.
Forgive me for doubting you're there,
Citizens, on your holodecks with earth wallpaper—

a shadow-toned ancestor with poorly pressed pants,
protected like a child from knowing the future.

# Early Spring

From my perspective, as a bird, everything seems the same
when I fly over your town. The little rectangles of your houses
are outlined in snow. I don't see praise or blame,
I see food, which I need full-time. Yesterday I came
up from another patchwork place, obeying some inside command
so basic it felt like an impulse, or free will. The small
flight plans—from branch to branch—are mine. I stand
where I stand, then I'm gone. And I forget it all,
though something in me remembers the larger strategy
that makes no sense, and doesn't have to. If I should fall
my feathers will disappear last of all. And the small beads
of brightness—my alert eyes—dim immediately,
so you'll know I'm gone. My song is complete, but clearly
part of an orchestra tuning up, and not yet here.

# Two Deer

Coming out of the shed
from fetching my son's
barbells—he's moving
and we command him
to take them—I see
two deer standing like
Christmas decorations, like
Christmas reindeer
beneath the linden tree
in the wintry light,
in the mid-morning light.
I want to be specific:
this is perhaps the fourth
sighting of deer here in
twenty-two years. We
raised our family, and even
our son's barbells
are leaving, and the deer
stood like a couple
poised to move in
or flee, depending.
I just kept walking
to see if the deer
might be surprised
by my not being surprised.
They didn't run this time.
Again, they stepped away,
visiting like forest gods,
undoubtedly a sign:
our daughter married,
our son and his barbells
moving to his own place,
a couple of deer browsing

for a moment in the yard,
naked as the day they first
came together to make
a family, Adam deer
and Eve deer, departing
silently, stepping
with ballet shoes
lightly through the brush
between our yard and
our neighbors'.

# A Weeping Cherry Tree

Though we were happy, we lay down awhile
beneath the weeping cherry tree and wept
while the woodchucks gathered round like mobile muffs

surfacing in our garden. It was spring and the small
pale pink blossoms hung from the tresses of the trees
and the music of the air danced in the penny pines

grown ponderous and lofty. On the soft earth,
damp still from spring rains, the sun accumulated
immaterially, like time, and the brave blades of the lawn

sang their green chorus when they could. A bride.
A groom. A river of ancestors without names,
like waves and particles of light flowing by us.

The tree held on to its enriched plot of earth, the fallen
apples of a thousand falls. The thin shadows
of the weeping branches laced the faces

of the couple who came to stand beneath it.
We wept and grew quiet, hoping the tree.
would tell us something. *I was grafted,*

said the tree, *so don't believe I grew this willowy.*
*I don't produce cherries. Trees that weep shouldn't*
*produce. Near where I'm standing there's a nest*

*of humans enjoying their brief century in the sun,*
*as I do. Waltz in close, my little ones.*
*If I'm sterile, I want to tell you my story,*

*I who mate fruitlessly, using the bees.*
*What I know of love is passive,*
*like limp hair. What you know pardons you*

*for not having a substantial root system. Graze*
*idly in time, my dear ones, like the plump bodies*
*of the woodchucks, their fur riffling in spring breezes.*

*Burrow into the earth as they do, chew the choicest tulip leaves.*
*I wouldn't say this to selfish or discourteous types,*
*but a tree learns to stand up for itself, a tree*

*learns to make its solitary statement. However intertwined,*
*life will insist on happening to you separately,*
*though who would know better than I*

*what it is to have one beloved object*
*always on the horizon. I confess that for me*
*it's the linden, the one you've chosen*

*for your canopy. That's why I'm weeping*
*in my temporary finery—neither jealous nor left out*
*but exactly where I am in sight of all*

*the day requires. You too will be adding*
*someone to all your day requires. At dawn,*
*birds will perch in your hair with their full throats*

*greeting the vague enormity of the Other.*
*Trees know. We don't get around much,*
*but we know, we have deep souls,*

*and a sense of being here. Light plays with us*
*just the way it plays with you. You rise.*
*You say hello. Or say nothing at all,*

*not alarmed to contemplate your rings*
*of annual growth. And when the leaves are out*
*the green bushy shapes dance, surrounded*

*by one spirit, which is how we think of the wind,*
*someone's breath that makes it seem we're breathing.*
*Not that we don't. Those clouds are our exhalations.*

*As we look at each other's thoughts,*
*the days pass, and grow enormous with age.*
*Yet there are always trees—like me—reticent,*

*more forceful with every turning, but still*
*trees with their wooden hearts, a heart*
*damp and green, unaccustomed to speaking.*

*for Rebecca Feldman and Brian Roessler*

# Spring

## 1. Flowers in Wartime

These daffodils in a blue vase, the ones my daughter gave us,
like old-fashioned telephones, their pretty flower faces
leaning outward in all directions, as though eager to save us
by collecting news: they come out of the night of their blue
vase, the inky light, and spread their curiosity,
their eager concern. *How is it in the world of men?*
they ask from the world of flowers. Their quick souls may be
pure, because their time's so brief, but they are here when
we call for them. They seem so centered, their symmetrical
faces with no ups or downs. They incline their heads
with momentary insight. *Remember color*, they tell us.
*Remember delicacy. Remember the fine little things*
*you may be neglecting, and sniff our petals. That's air*
*from another planet. Don't you like it better?*

## 2. Car Ride, First Day of Spring

Dan and I leave late for synagogue. Why does he go?
Because his girlfriend (who goes to church) approves.
But on the ride over, the gray pelt of the woods showing
the first red tinge of spring, he talks about moving
up to Vermont (where *she* lives) and I reply
by suggesting he might consider therapy. No,
he says, he wouldn't want to tell her. No guile,
no secrets. In our synagogue's loft, a circle of gray heads
explore the branches of mystical texts, the more minds
the better. *Godliness begins in humility*. That said,
how does it apply? On the ride back, do I try to find
a way to persuade him, or practice the small courtesy of silence,
and give him a chance to breathe, to think? The air says,
*He'll survive, even if he moves up there.*

## 3. A Visit from the Tree Man

Easy to understand how Chekhov's characters must feel
when we survey our yard with Pavel, the tree man,
and he shows us the cedar hit by lightning, its bark peeled,
or the crab apple, hollowed out, ready to slam
into the house in a strong north wind. Our strength is failing,
our years are numbered, and now even the trees
are aging and need care. We stand here hailing
our posterity. We're sorry to leave you these
acres of dead wood and scrambled branches. It's true
old trees bloom with heartbreaking loveliness. So we
struggle, in our feeble way, as you will. Like you
we wished for a simpler life than this one turned out to be,
and yet feel grateful for the spring, each time it appears,
and plant a few saplings that won't look good for years.

## 4. An Errand

Approaching the bank, with its mulched plantings, its instant
strip mall landscaping, I feel once more that I'm reliving
an errand my father must have done for me. I can't
remember the specifics. But once again I'm giving
money to my son. I'm cheerful with the young teller
when she tells me it will hit his account today.
He's somewhere up north. His new landlord, a fellow
who works in construction, has asked Dan to pay
first and last month's rent. I can see the check
in Dan's crab-like writing in that man's hand
and it's a good check. It hasn't bounced. Indirectly
it's like a letter from me. I'm sure my dad did this errand
dozens of times. Making deposits. The sums
forgotten. Incalculable. He'd sign, and it was done.

## 5. Travel

"Going on Nan's painting trip?" her student asks.
She's staring hard at me, as though she'd like to come along—
while I'm mostly nervous, I tell her. This feeling lasts
till departure: like preparing for death. The wrong
attitude, I know. Terrible to be so self-delighting
I don't want to leave my reading chair, or the screen
of my computer. And just now the garden is fighting
for my attention, the cherries like veiled brides, the peonies
shooting up near the door, their buds the size of marbles
waiting to unfold—after we're gone. Aunt Molly
loved them, and now so do I, and I recall the marvel
of their thick old-lady perfume, and think of the folly
of travel. "Packing," I explain. "We'll get through it.
Married to Picasso," I shrug, wondering why I do it.

## 6. Final Affairs

I leave a note on the kitchen table, not to be opened
unless Something Bad happens. Each departure
reminds us of the big one, I guess. Yet it feels dopey
to be addressing my kids from beyond my grave, sure
they'll be feeling traumatized, an upheaval in their universe,
as when my mother quietly, predictably passed away
and the still-unexpected call divided my life, irreversibly.
On one side, I had a mother, someone who would say
mother sorts of things to me—since her flesh used to enclose me—
and on the other side the naked silence of an orphan.
"What did you write?" Nan asks. "Oh. About the key
to the safe deposit, and how, if they retrieve our bodies, we'd planned
on Edgell Grove—unless you want that spot in the Jura, above a
      valley?"
"No," she nods. "I like to think of people visiting me."

## 7. Real Estate

"So if someone gave us—" and here she names an astronomical
     sum—
for our house, "what would we do?" She wants my opinion?
We're walking through our garden, but we've recently come
from synagogue, part of the faithful minion
studying the law. Sabbatical. Jubilee.
The house isn't ours, anyway—that was this morning's teaching—
that neither space, nor time, nor even sovereignty
over the self, are really ours. I guess we're reaching
the age where we know that, but still our borrowed trees
reach heavenward into the blue sky that's been loaned to us,
along with our will to be together. Down on her knees
in the flower patch, weeding, this world that's been shown to us
is enough, she tells me. "Maybe you have a thirst
to wander. But I have lifetimes to spend here first."

# Letter from My Working Self
# to My Resting Self

You are far away, in some confined little box,
like an image on a TV screen. Like a commercial
for life insurance, in your beachcomber garb,

a man at peace, staring at the sea, which clashes
with the rocks, the beach itself, but never toils,
and you are in an Eden with no future, only

a premonition. No one will remember you, your footprints
erased, smoothed over by the tide, while I
inspire and offend and press myself into the history of these minds

that scan the future, hoping for the advent
of some remarkable light. While I am lost in toil,
combing sentences tangled as seaweed, you are lost

in a coastal dream, on the edge of being, the shadows
steeper each time you measure them, the waves
creeping nearer your feet. When you speak,

you speak to yourself, no one around to stare at you,
and you can hear everything you're thinking,
if you call those thoughts, those registrations of phenomena,

while you float, unanchored, in an unchanging surf,
as though you were featureless and legless as an oyster
or stand watch, mysteriously impulsive as a bird.

How we came from the same mother I don't know,
I a tiller of the soil, you a shepherd of clouds,
like a bodiless soul no one knows about,

who might be anywhere, under your straw hat,
or rippling the water in a fleeting cat's paw, like a stroke
of darker, grainier blue on the pale blue of the bay.

# Grayness

At home Nan and her friend Joanie
are drawing in our kitchen.
"I'm going to live," I tell them.
"They aren't lymph nodes. It's not
lymphoma. These are nothing but
submaxillary salivary glands. How
could my doctor not *know*? How
dumb would you have to be
in my field? This *might* be
a Shakespearean sonnet, but
I'll have to send you to a *specialist*?"

That gets a laugh, and since I'm going to live
I make myself lunch. "It's not
like the body keeps changing its mind
about where things are. It's *anatomy*.
The ENT doc felt my neck once."

Yes, yes, they agree, their drawings
spread colorfully over large sheets
of white. Anything can be included.
The light fixture. My yellow coat
I wear when sailing on gray days.
Suddenly, this vast future, like the sea
unfolds, and I have to cross it.
I have to drink more fluids.

Otherwise, I can work on a poem.
I don't need to be part of this conversation.
With a mind like mine I can imagine
people might begin to call me "brave,"
the horizon shrinking in little increments
to the railings of a special bed.

I'll start with my thoughts
driving home from the clinic,
my death revoked. *The pond's
still here, and the road, also gray,
precious with traffic. And then
in the kitchen, two women
with their bright drawings,
talking.*

# The Couple at the Window

*after a drawing by George Tooker*

Whatever it is they are watching
down below—she with her large arms
folded on the sill, he with his arm
raised above her, as if to grasp the edge
of the window frame—whatever
it is that seems to be lighting their faces,
their similar faces, rounded, with eyes
half-lidded, arouses in them
a similar compassion, as if love
has made their faces look alike
(the man has no shirt, the woman
possibly just an undergarment)
or they are simply siblings
from the human family, spectators
high above the street, who may be
similarly saddened, but softly so,
by the lighting of the lamps at evening—
whatever it is they are watching
must be better off for being watched,
as we are when our parents watch us,
even when they've left us, their shapes
becoming rounded like passing clouds,
a couple at a window above the world,
so easy in their guardianship of whatever
drifts before them at the end of evening,
as if it had become their own child
playing beneath them on the street.

# After Watching Twyla Tharp

The curled leaves are struggling into green, and from green
into fullness. Trees that cast speckled shade
soon will cast black shadows. At night I dream
the moment in my boat when I cast off the mooring pennant
and motor out through the green arms of the land
onto the dazzling, free-form water, rising
with each tide as my wife's side rises with each breath
beneath the covers at night. I think of the brain
prickling with the tiny pin-point lights of the day
like phosphorescent seaweed in the dark. It needs a flood
to carry it into sleep, the way the world needs sun
for two or three days for all the buds to open.
We wake, blink, and everything's green with spring,
the way the body, sick for a month, rises one morning
as comfortable with itself as if the flesh were cool silk.
*If the movement feels good to do, then probably*
*it looks good to others.* Wearing my flesh lightly
I kneel to press the kill switch on the motor
and the boat keeps bubbling forward inside the wind
as if it doesn't know any better, has forgotten its mass,
its iron keels—bubbling forward, at a slight heel,
bow foaming—and where is the mind in all this?
Like a small passenger on board the body which follows
its will, which is also the will of the wind.
From land you'll see the white sail's progress
against the curve of Great Island, slow
but inexorable, the way the tide darkens the sand,
or the way clouds drift floating south.
The tip of the sail is like the pointer on a gauge,
which says time is filling up with life till it's full,
the way the sail is full, and begins to move.
Somewhere. Be patient. Enjoy the feeling of this flesh.

The Felix Pollak Prize in Poetry
The University of Wisconsin Press Poetry Series
Ronald Wallace, General Editor

*Now We're Getting Somewhere* ❖ David Clewell
Henry Taylor, Judge, 1994

*The Legend of Light* ❖ Bob Hicok
Carolyn Kizer, Judge, 1995

*Fragments in Us: Recent and Earlier Poems* ❖ Dennis Trudell
Philip Levine, Judge, 1996

*Don't Explain* ❖ Betsy Sholl
Rita Dove, Judge, 1997

*Mrs. Dumpty* ❖ Chana Bloch
Donald Hall, Judge, 1998

*Liver* ❖ Charles Harper Webb
Robert Bly, Judge, 1999

*Ejo* ❖ Derick Burleson
Alicia Ostriker, Judge, 2000

*Borrowed Dress* ❖ Cathy Colman
Mark Doty, Judge, 2001

*Ripe* ❖ Roy Jacobstein
Edward Hirsch, Judge, 2002

*The Year We Studied Women* ❖ Bruce Snider
Kelly Cherry, Judge, 2003

*A Sail to Great Island* ❖ Alan Feldman
Carl Dennis, Judge, 2004